THE
Archive Photographs
SERIES

BOGNOR REGIS

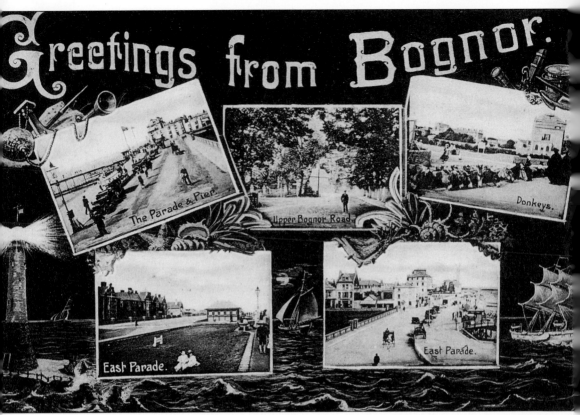

GREETINGS FROM BOGNOR. A multi-view card, posted in 1909. There were many such cards produced for almost every town and even villages, but this one with its embellishment of nautical subjects is more imaginative than most. The message on the reverse starts us off well with 'This is a lovely place . . . something like Weymouth'.

THE
Archive Photographs
SERIES

BOGNOR REGIS

Compiled by
Tony Wales

CHALFORD

First published 1997
Copyright © Tony Wales, 1997

The Chalford Publishing Company
St Mary's Mill, Chalford,
Stroud, Gloucestershire, GL6 8NX

ISBN 0 7524 1035 0

Typesetting and origination by
The Chalford Publishing Company
Printed in Great Britain by
Bailey Print, Dursley, Gloucestershire

*In memory of my aunt Bel, who with a little help from Gerard Young,
sparked my lifelong interest in Sussex literature.*

Bognor Regis, sea-side town,
Awarded 'Regis' by the Crown,
Nestling by the sea so fair,
With its climate warm and rare.
Hotham's dream was of a place,
Ordered well and fair of face.
So it was for many a year;
Then came Butlin with his gear.
Hotham's ghost turned in his grave,
As thousands came for coastal rave.
Beauty gone and vision lost,
Now its residents count the cost.
'Turn back the clock!' that cannot be;
But oh! If councillors could only see,
The folly of their past mistakes,
Their tears would fill a thousand lakes.
'The future's ours', we're always told;
Please let authority now be BOLD;
For Bognor can be fair of face,
Given planning of good grace.
Hotham's vision has not died,
Bognor still has much of pride.
Let us rise then to the task,
And in its beauty once more bask.

(© Peter J. Millam, 1996)

Contents

I HAVE JUST ARRIVED AT BOGNOR

HAVE JUST ARRIVED. This was a card posted on 30 August 1907, when seaside holidays were still a novelty and worthy of note with a card such as this. The message on the back adds 'Arrived safely', although it seems the sender had travelled just the few miles from Shoreham, along the coast. This bright comic card is typical of such productions, which were printed with the name left blank, so this could be added before they were put on sale.

Acknowledgements

Books of this sort are always a combined effort on the part of the main compiler and many other kind people who give of their time and knowledge and not least the loan of pictures and postcards. In this case I would particulary like to single out for thanks Ms K. Shakespeare and Ms K. Balaam, of the Chichester Institute of Higher Education, Bognor Regis Campus Library, who allowed me to browse amongst, and subsequently make copies of, some of the treasures in the Gerard Young Collection of photographs. As always, I am also greatly indebted to Mr M. Hayes and Mr R. Knibb of the West Sussex County Library. Also to Mr David Turner who copied many of the borrowed photographs and to Ms Sylvia Endacott for her tremendous assistance and encouragement.

I am also grateful to all of the following for their help in many different ways: Mr J. Cannon; Miss M. Carrington; Chichester Reference Library; Mr C.W. Cramp; Miss D. Fernee; Mrs D. Howard; Mr R. Iden; Lens of Sutton; Miss W. Luxton; Mrs S.A. Mann; Revd P.J. Millam; Mr J. Muggeridge; Mr E. Pollington; Mr F. Robinson; Mr and Mrs J. Sykes; Mrs P. A. Thrussell; Mrs M. Tippen.

If I have forgotton anyone, may I sincerely apologise.

A word about dating: it is often difficult to decide on a date for a photograph when no details are available. If you know that I have got it wrong, please correct me.

Tony Wales has written widely on Sussex and his books include *We Wunt be Druv* (1976), *A Sussex Garland* (1979), *The West Sussex Village Book* (1984), *Sussex Customs, Curiosities and Country Lore* (1990), *Sussex Ghosts and Legends* (1992), *The Landscapes of West Sussex* (1994) and *Brighton and Hove* (1997) in the Archive Photographs Series.

Introduction

My early memories of Bognor centre round a few pleasant days out with my parents and a bucket and spade. A rather more intimate relationship with the town developed after my Aunt moved to Rose Green, near Aldwick in the mid 1930s. It was in her seaside bungalow that I spent many happy weekends with her and my cousin, who was four years older than me. Money was short, so we almost always walked into Bognor, choosing different routes and invariably making the walk an adventure. It was at this time that my Aunt, who knew the local author Gerard Young, introduced me to his books which he was lovingly writing about Flansham, where he had his cottage in Hoe Lane. She bought them all for me as they appeared, asking the author to inscribe them to me. These were my first Sussex books, beginning a lifelong interest in Sussex literature.

Later I learnt more about the town and its rather unusual history. Bognor began at just a few fishermen's huts on the seashore, within sight of the once celebrated Bognor Rocks. There were also the twin villages of Bersted, a little inland. It was to this unpromising beginning that a rich London hat maker, Richard Hothman, decided to graft a completely new seaside town, which he planned to call Hothamton. This was 1787 and he built his houses in the style of the time: simple and of local brick. Richard's dreams were by no means completely fulfilled by the time he died in 1799 and in spite of his enthusiasm and apparent success, there was insufficient money left after his demise for the grand plan to be completed and Bognor then developed in a much more piecemeal fashion.

Over the years the town was visited by many bastions of society, including members of the Royal family, but it never succeeded in becoming quite the regal place that many of its residents desired. It was not until 1929 when a most unlikely event took place, and King George V came to Craigweil House, close to Aldwick, for his convalescence after a serious illness that it became undoubtedly royal, with the addition of Regis to its name.

Bognor has had a mixed press through the years. It has been described variously as 'Royal, rural and respectable'; 'The Spinster of the South Coast, rather than a Queen, like Brighton, or an Empress like Worthing'; 'Dear Little Bognor' (by Queen Victoria); and, more unkindly, 'A Jumble of a resort'. Perhaps the most telling remark was made before the First World War when someone said that 'Visiting Bognor was rather like going to Church'.

In modern times, Bognor, with all its joys and tribulations, has been well documented by several authors, but the man to whom I must return is of course Gerard Young, who began to write the definitive history of the town, but sadly died before completing it. His brother completed this most readable book and I have to record my deep debt to it and to the earlier happenings mentioned at the start of this Introduction.

The modern poem which appears on page 4 was written by a Bognor poet, and says in rhyme much of what I would wish to say in the pictures and prose that follow.

Bibliography

Baber, Terry G: *Bognor Regis Now and Then*. 1988.
Beswick, M: *Brickmaking in Sussex*. 1993.
Bognor Regis: *A Brief Guide to Places of Interest*. 1981.
Butler, Charles: *Inns, Taverns and Hotels Past and Present of Bognor Regis*. 1993.
Cartland, James: *Bygone Bognor*. 1979
Davis, J.B.: *The Origin and Description of Bognor or Hothampton*. 1907.
Endacott, Sylvia: *'Our Mary'*. 1987.
Endacott, Sylvia: *Bognor Regis in Old Picture Postcards*. 1993.
Endacott, Sylvia: *Glimpses of Bognor Regis*, 1985.
Gowler, Michael A.H.: *The Poor of Bognor. 1790-1870*. 1994.
Harmer, Rob: *Bognor Regis in Old Photographs*. 1989.
Hudson, Tim and Ann: *Felpham by the Sea*. 1988.
Jordan, S.: *The Bognor Branch Line*. 1989.
Jordan, S.: *Gone to Blazes*. 1995.
Lee, Judith M.: *Private Schools in Bognor Regis & District 1860-1960*. 1983.
Mills, Vanessa: *Bognor Regis, A Pictorial History*. 1995.
Montgomery, John: *History, People and Places in West Sussex*. 1977.
Nairn, Ian and Nikolaus Pevsner: *The Buildings of England. Sussex*. 1965.
Nesse, Neville: *Bognor of the Past*. 1983.
Ogley, B., I. Currie and M. Davison: *The Sussex Weather Book*. 1991.
Parry, J.D.: *The Coast of Sussex*. 1833.
Rees, Josephine Duggan: Slindon. *A Portrait of a Sussex Village*. 1988.
Venables, E.M. and A.F. Outen: *Building Stones of Old Bognor*. 1969.
Warden, S. and D. Arscott: *Hidden Sussex - The Towns*. 1990.
Wells, Paul and Sylvia Endacott: *Glimpses of Bognor Pier*. 1990.
Young, Gerard: *A History of Bognor Regis*. 1983.
Young, Gerard: *The Chronicle of a Country Cottage*. 1942.
Young, Gerard: *Come into the Country*. 1943.
Young, Gerard: *The Cottage in the Fields*. 1945.
Young, Gerard: *Down Hoe Lane*. 1950.
Various newspapers, magazines, maps and guide books.

One
Sea and Sands

BOGNOR FROM THE AIR.(4395)

BOGNOR FROM THE AIR, 1920s. As flight became commonplace, so aerial photographs appeared on picture postcards. This is a card posted in June 1922 to Newcastle, from Mill House, Bognor. It reads, 'Dear Madam. I shall be able to get you a bedroom for the first and second week. Will try and give you one in the house if possible.' One wonders what the alternative would have been.

CHILDREN PADDLING, *c.* 1904. Youngsters have always enjoyed the sands at Bognor, which are noted for their smoothness. They also love to hunt for unusual pebbles and shells. In the past, the poorer children collected nodules of iron pyrates (known as 'Thunderbolts') which could be sold at threepence a bushel in Chichester. Later, these were sold by adults to coal merchants as a source of sulphuric acid, fetching one and sixpence a hundredweight.

DONKEYS AND GOAT CART, *c.* 1909. Mr Dick Neale kept a string of donkeys, which were very much a part of Bognor seafront at this period. The writer of the card has drawn attention to the 'portrait of self and brothers on t'other side'.

EAST PARADE AND BEACH, early 1900s. This shows some of the ungainly big-wheeled bathing huts, which were such a distinctive adjunct to the sea and sands in Victorian and Edwardian days. One of the horses which was used to haul the huts down to the water can be seen.

THE BOAT SLIP AND BATHING HUTS. A picture from a similar period to the one above. In the previous century, a book on Bognor said, 'The machines are ready at six o'clock and the conductor is waiting till twelve or one. There are ten or twelve machines at Bognor, which are drawn to any depth required; at low water the bather may go even as far as the rocks; the ladies will find a female guide'. Obviously, the number of machines increased as time went on. The rocks mentioned were the famous Bognor Rocks which hemmed the coastline.

CHILDREN'S PLAYGROUND, early in this century. Children were particularly happy at Bognor, as the sands were so suitable for all kinds of play. There were also entertainers on the beach, as can be seen in this picture (and in the Fun and Games section of this book). Occasionally unusual attractions appeared, such as the turtle which was washed ashore in 1860 and ended up as soup at the Claremont Hotel.

OPEN AIR CONCERT, c. 1909. Adults and children gather in front of The Royal Pier Hotel for a show by one of the many seaside entertainers working in Bognor at this time. The adults and even the children seem very overdressed by today's standards. The Fountain, erected to commemorate Queen Victoria's Diamond Jubilee, can be seen in the background opposite The Steyne.

THE WESTERN BANDSTAND. A picture from the 1920s, of the site of Bognor's first bandstand. This is an improved version, as the original had been built here in 1901 at a cost of a mere £60. As can be seen, the voluminous fashions of the previous century were giving way to slightly less long and more simple styles. Eventually this was to become the location of the Esplanade Band Enclosure and Theatre.

THE EASTERN BANDSTAND. Another picture from around the 1920s. This bandstand was built in 1910, rivalling the earlier one at the other end of the promenade. It was removed during the Second World War and replaced in 1948 by another bought from Cheltenham. A Military band are entertaining the visitors here, possibly that of the Royal Sussex Regiment. Their regimental marching song was the famous 'Sussex by the Sea', which was written by William Ward-Higgs, a resident of Bognor, in 1907. He penned the familiar tune when his favourite niece, Gladys, became engaged to Captain Waithman of the 2nd Battalion. Ward-Higgs lived at Hollywood House, South Bersted, from 1902 until 1908.

THE BAND ENCLOSURE, WESTERN PROMENADE, late 1930s. With the removal of the old bandstand, a grand scheme to build a Winter Garden was mooted, but the town council jibbed at the cost and a band (or orchestral) enclosure was provided instead. It was opened in June 1937, with a concert by the Bognor Regis Municipal Orchestra.

THE ESPLANADE CONCERT HALL, 1940s. Not satisfied with the Band Enclosure, the council revamped the building in 1946/7 and it became The Esplanade Concert Hall, or Theatre. During the Summer, concert parties entertained the visitors with daily shows. I remember an incident from my teenage years: I attended one of these shows by myself and was invited onto the stage by a very large blonde lady, who proceeded to embarrass me by sitting on my knee and planting a huge kiss on my cheek. The evidence was still very much apparent when I returned to my Aunt's bungalow, much to her amusement. Luckily, my mother was twenty-five miles away, or I would have had a very different reception.

PLEASURE BOATS, 1920s. Very much an important part of a summer holiday at Bognor, these were the small boats which took trippers out for a quick sea trip, leaving from the beach via portable walkways, which were extended as the tide moved out. One of these boats just had to be called *The Skylark*.

EAST PARADE. A delightfully relaxed picture from early this century. The ladies are still wearing long skirts, ornate hats, and carrying sunshades. Even the dog looks suitably decorous. In the background can be seen the two convalescent homes which had been recently opened. Also the Mackonochie Home run by Miss Louisa Stewart as a holiday home for the clergy. Perhaps the one jarring note is the fisherman's boat, showing that Bognor was still a working town.

WESTERN PROMENADE AND BEACH, 1930s. Children and adults are a little less restrained by elaborate clothes than in some of the earlier photographs, but a comment on the sort of visitors who were attracted to Bognor at this period is provided by the array of invalid carriages and expensive prams parked along the Prom.

Royal Pier Hotel, Bognor.

ROYAL PIER HOTEL, c. 1913. One of the many fine hotels which were a feature of Bognor at this time. However, the writer of the card was not actually staying at this hotel, but apparently at a boarding house. She comments that Mrs I. had sprained her ankle last week and Charlie his this week - but this seemingly did not prevent them from attending a performance of *Gypsy Love*, which they enjoyed.

EAST PARADE AND AMUSEMENT ARCADES, late 1930s. A relatively modern photograph showing what had happened to the Eastern end of Bognor's promenade by this time. Billy Butlin had arrived with his amusements and what's more, imitation rocks housing a miniature zoo. Not to everyone's taste, of course, but as a youngster I loved it. The opening of the zoo was arranged for Wednesday 5 July 1933 and either by luck or good management, the newspapers reported that a lion on its way to the new zoo had escaped whilst being transported from Butlin's existing zoo at Skegness. There was the expected scare and the grand opening was postponed, as the police combed the area for the missing animal. Then a sheep was reported dead and mauled near Pagham, which just added to the local's fears. So Bognor's new zoo and what was to be its most famous resident, became front page news over the whole country. However, things were not exactly as they seemed; in fact, the group of animals travelling from Skegness had not actually included a lion at all. But Mr Butlin was equal to the situation. He quickly obtained a lion from a zoo at Maidstone and then announced that his escaped animal had been recaptured with no loss of life. The story of Billy Butlin's lion has now become part of Bognor folk-lore. However, amusements and zoo animals were not all that Bognor had to offer. In the left hand bottom area of the picture can be seen a group of local 'sailors', probably waiting for the tide to be right for them to operate their pleasure boat.

'LOVE IN IDLENESS'. Postcard sent on Saturday 19 September 1911. The poetic printed message reads: 'Come unto these silvery sands at Bognor'. The 'Bognor' has probably been added to what was a standard seaside card. The written message on the card assured the recipient that the sender had arrived safely and that Mother and Auntie were waiting at Barnham Junction. The message concluded with the assurance that: 'We are just off for some fun, for the weather is lovely'.

FLOODS, c. 1930. This was no novelty to Bognor folk, who were quite used to this kind of scene in York Road down to the sea front. The Theatre Royal is on the left and there is a seemingly superfluous 10 mile speed limit sign.

HIGH SEAS, early 1900s. A typical card of rough weather at Bognor, welcomed at least by the local photographers, Webster and Webb of the High Street. How did they manage to persuade the spectators to stand so near to the waves? Or are we a little cynical in thinking that the picture was 'posed'?

Storm Scene, Bognor.

STORM SCENE, 1920s. This kind of weather is not unusual at Bognor. For instance, in 1935, a storm hit the town, which swept away the bathing huts and deck chairs and reduced them to driftwood, leaving the shore strewn with wreckage.

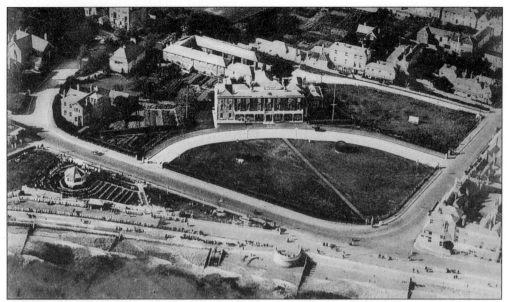

THE ROYAL NORFOLK HOTEL FROM THE AIR, 1930s. Nobody seems to know how it got its 'Royal', but it has been known as this since the 1880s and the hotel is very proud of its coat of arms. It began life as a small inn, which was destroyed by fire, together with a group of cottages in 1826. The fire was brought under control with the help of a detachment of the Scots Fusiliers from Bognor Barracks. In 1830 a new hotel was built on the present site and the balcony added in the 1880s. Coaches stopped at The Royal Norfolk Hotel arriving in time for tea.

THE ROYAL NORFOLK HOTEL, 1920s. This classic Regency-style hotel has played host through the years to a great many distinguished guests, including Napoleon III, Queen Alexandra and her sister, the Empress Maud of Russia, Queen Victoria, Edward VII and Solly Joel, the 'Diamond King'. As a boy I remember being solemnly instructed by an ancient inhabitant, that the rocks which could be seen at low tide, were the remains of the original hotel, before the sea washed it away.

THE KURSAAL, 1900s. This attractive building was opened in 1911, although the German-sounding name was dropped in the 1914/18 war. At different times it included a skating rink, dance hall, a cinema, Pierrotland and Constitution Club. In 1919 it became known as The Theatre Royal, although the name Pierrotland also survived. The theatre seated 1,000 and Jack Hylton and Tommy Handley appeared there, arriving for performances each day on their cycles. Later in the 1970s it was refurbished, becoming the Rex Entertainment Centre, with a restaurant, ballroom and theatre. This was demolished in 1975, to be later succeeded by the Bognor Regis Centre in 1980.

BOGNOR PIER. An early picture showing the pier unembellished with buildings. It was originally built in 1865, a slim iron structure, jutting 1,000 feet into the sea and costing £5,000. In 1883 the admission charge was one penny. In 1900 the sea and pavilion was added and in 1903 a landing stage for paddle steamers. The most famous piermaster was Mr John Smith, who held the post for 25 years. On the day of his funeral the pier was closed and the blinds in the town were drawn.

BOGNOR PIER. A picture from a glass plate negative, c. 1900. In 1908 the pier was sold for ten shillings and the new owner added a theatre (seating 1,180), a cinema, a skating rink and an arcade at the shore end. During storms in 1964 and 1965 most of the seaward part of the pier disappeared into the sea, but the entrance buildings still remain and plans have been discussed to restore it to its former glory. A former Council chairman said: 'Bognor without its pier, is like strawberries without cream'.

THE PIER, BOGNOR.

BOGNOR PIER. A picture from the 1920s showing some of the charabancs which plied their trade each day from this spot, visiting Sussex beauty spots and also the famous Bognor Stamp House. From 1910/11, the new owner spent nearly £30,000 in widening the shore end and in building a theatre, cinema and twelve shops. He said one of his most profitable ventures was in building the arcade, where trippers could shelter from the rain. Mary Wheatland, Bognor's famous bathing lady, ran her business from the tiny striped hut on the left of the picture.

BOGNOR PIER, early 1900s. This picture shows the Pier Theatre and Cinema. In the foreground is a beach vendor (probably selling ice-cream) doing good business. During the First World War, 200 soldiers were billeted on the pier. In the Second World War it became H.M.S. *Barbara*, a naval observation post.

"WORTHING BELLE"

Will make the following Trips (Weather and Circumstances permitting)

SUNDAY, JULY 28th.	WEDNESDAY, JULY 31st.
WORTHING & Back (Twice).	**NEWHAVEN & SEAFORD BAY.**
Morning Trip.	West P. 11.0, Palace P. 11.10, Bk. 12 50
Palace P. 11.0, West P. 11.10, Bk. 12 50	**WORTHING and**
Afternoon Trip.	**LITTLEHAMPTON.**
Palace P. 2.50, West P. 3.0, Bk. 3 40	Palace Pier 2.45, West Pier 2.55,
CHANNEL TRIP, 6d.	Worthing 3.40.
Palace P. 7.10, West P. 7.20, Bk. 8.30	Returning from Littlehampton 5.15, Worthing 6.0, Bk. 1 at Brighton 6.45.
	Note Cheap Return Fares
MONDAY, JULY 29th.	Brighton to Littlehampton 1/6 only
GRAND ALL-DAY TRIP TO	**CHANNEL TRIP, 6d.**
WORTHING, LITTLEHAMPTON	Palace P. 7.10, West P. 7.20, Bk. 8.30
and BOGNOR.	
Palace Pier 10.50, West Pier 11.0,	THURSDAY, AUGUST 1st.
Worthing 11.50, Littlehampton 12.40.	**Towards LITTLEHAMPTON.**
Returning from Bognor 3.30, Little-	Palace P. 11.0, West P. 11.10, Bk. 12.50
hampton, 4.20, Worthing 5.10.	**WORTHING & BOGNOR.**
Back at Brighton 6.0.	Palace P. 2.45, West P. 2.55,
Return Fares: Brighton to Worthing, 1/6.	Worthing 3.40. Return from Bognor 5.30
Brighton to Littlehampton, 2/-.	Worthing 6.30. Back at Brighton 7.20.
Brighton to Bognor, 2/6.	Brighton to Worthing 1/6 1st Cl., 1/- 2nd.
CHANNEL TRIP, 6d.	,, Bognor 2/- ,, 1/6 ,,
Palace P. 7.10, West P. 7.20, Bk. 8.30	**CHANNEL TRIP, 6d.**
	West P. 7.30, Palace P. 7.40, Bk. 8.40
TUESDAY, JULY 30th.	
WORTHING & Back (Twice).	FRIDAY, AUGUST 2nd.
Morning Trip.	**NEWHAVEN & SEAFORD BAY.**
Palace P. 11.0, West P. 11.10, Bk. 1.0	West P. 10.50, Palace P. 11.5, Bk. 12.50
Afternoon Trip.	**WORTHING & Back.**

THE WORTHING BELLE, c. 1900s. A poster advertising this and other paddle steamers which collected passengers from the end of Bognor's pier, taking in Brighton, Worthing and Littlehampton (weather and circumstances permitting). Prices were surprisingly cheap. A Channel Trip cost only sixpence and other fares ranged from one to two shillings.

PADDLE STEAMER AT PIER HEAD, 1900s. Piers were built originally as landing stages for boats, so it was no unusual sight to see a steamer picking up holidaymakers from Bognor's pier. Steamers who used the pier included *The Worthing Belle*, *Princess May* and *The Brighton Queen*. The boy in the then-popular sailor suit is apparently being hurried along by his father, perhaps to catch the boat.

THE WEST PARADE AND PIER, early 1900s. The Edwardian mamas and their offspring look, as usual in this period, a trifle overdressed for the seaside. Perhaps some of the youngsters on the prom are wishing they could join the less controlled boys and girls on the beach below.

JUST ARRIVED, GOING STRONG. A postcard from June 1929. The postcard manufacturers were running out of ideas and decided to take a perfectly innocent card showing Waterloo Square and the Pier and add a cartoon-like character. Well, there's no accounting for taste!

HOORAY FOR A HOLIDAY AT BOGNOR. Another of the cards produced so that any seaside town's name could be added. Even the flag looks as if it has been superimposed, so perhaps this card was also sold to resorts abroad. Bognor has always been known for its smooth, soft sand, so its popularity for sand castle making is not in any doubt, as I recall from my own childhood. In the 1930s a sand artist, Samuel Mather, known as 'The Sand Scratcher', drew lovely pictures of famous castles, hoping that holidaymakers would appreciate them sufficiently to put something in his collecting tin. He died aged 83 in 1960. It has been seriously suggested that *Sanditon*, the novel on which Jane Austen was working when she died, may have been based on Bognor. So perhaps the smooth sands gave her the idea for the title.

Two
Town and Around

orian Convalescent Home, Surrey House, Bognor Regis.

VICTORIAN CONVALESCENT HOME, SURREY HOUSE, 1930s. HRH Princess Mary, Duchess of Teck (who died in 1898) maintained a small home for poor women from the East End of London, near Richmond. HRH The Duchess of York (later Queen Mary) wished to continue this work and she founded a home of rest for poor working women of London, at Bognor. The home was opened on Monday 9 June 1900, together with the Victorian Convalescent Home for Surrey Women, at the Eastern end of the Front. This was a great occasion for the town, with many notables invited and a Guard of Honour provided by the Royal Sussex Regiment.

The Sitting Room, Victorian Convalescent Home, Surrey House, Bognor Regis.

THE SITTING ROOM, VICTORIAN CONVALESCENT HOME, SURREY HOUSE, soon after its opening in 1900. 9 July 1900 was a great day for Bognor with the visit of HRH The Duchess of York to perform the opening ceremonies of the two homes, accompanied by an array of other dignitaries. The parade through the town included representatives of the Volunteer Fire Brigade; the Coast Guard Service; the carriages with their Royal Highnesses and three other carriages with local councillors. An archway built by local fishermen was erected near the homes and the same evening the new £2,000 Pavilion at the end of the Pier was opened. A special train travelled from Victoria for the event. As well as the main ceremony, there was a service conducted by the Lord Bishop of Rochester and a musical programme by the Band of the 2nd Volunteer Battalion of the Royal Sussex Regiment. A fine luncheon was provided for the guests, with a menu in French.

The Garden. Victorian Convalescent Home, Surrey House, Bognor.

THE GARDEN, THE VICTORIAN CONVALESCENT HOME. A picture from 1914 showing staff and patients. The message on the reverse of the postcard says: 'Am going out this morning, on the Pier to hear a concert. We can go when we like, but must go out with the women at the Home'.

THE ENTRANCE OF SURREY HOUSE. Bognor is said to have had several haunted houses. One of these was apparently the Victorian Convalescent Home, which had a fairly harmless ghost who provided some thumps and bumps in the night and also wafted cigarette smoke through the rooms. Presumably, cigarette smoking was not encouraged, but some patients may have had an illicit puff, which could have accounted for the latter phenomenon.

In Commemoration
of the
Sixty Years of Her Majesty's Reign,
June 1837=1897.

BY PERMISSION OF MESSRS. GRAVES, PALL MALL

The Victorian
Convalescent Home
for . .
Surrey Women
at Bognor.

FRONT PAGE OF BROCHURE produced for Queen Vicoria's Diamond Jubilee, by The Victorian Convalescent Home for Surrey Women, when it was still in its original site in a house in London Road. Miss M. Carrington who provided me with a great many details on the homes, said that Miss Routledge, the Matron for 20 years, used to hold big parties for local people. All the patients were sent to bed early on these occasions. When Miss Routledge retired in 1920, there were 80 applicants for her job.

THE STEYNE, *c.* 1906. An 1833 guide described it thus: 'An oblong space open to the sea, neat and cheerful, including the Chapel of Ease and a small market'. The name almost certainly refers to 'Stone', and perhaps was borrowed from Brighton. A newspaper report from 1897 mentions an accident in The Steyne caused by the handles of a truck which stood close to the railings being caught up with a cab. This resulted in Mr Florence of Landsdowne Mews falling on his head and being badly injured. This picture shows a truck near the railings - was it perhaps the same one which featured in this report?

THE STEYNE. An undated picture from early this century, showing a typical perambulator and possibly a nanny. The Steyne was developed as a fashionable area between 1820 and 1840. Many celebrities stayed in the houses here, including Lewis Carroll and Gertrude Lawrence. The railings were removed in the Second World War, including a milestone which read '7 miles to Chichester Cross'.

THE MERCHANT TAYLOR'S CONVALESCENT HOME, near the High Street, early in this century. This was formerly known as East Row, and included six houses built by Richard Hotham. The building was faced with white stucco, provided by cement from the old mill in Nyewood Lane. It was opened by the Merchant Taylors in 1870 as a convalescent home for men and later extended to the neighbouring terrace to provide a home for women. Convalescent homes such as this increased during the inter-war years, making the town a little less popular with the aristocracy.

THE MERCHANT TAILOR'S LADIES HOME, c. 1907. The spelling of the home's name varied. In 1955 the two homes were acquired by developers and, although listed, they were demolished to make way for the Queensway Development. The chapel survived for a few more years (see page 66).

CHARLWOOD STREET. Possibly 1930s or later. This is in the Victoria Park area of Bognor, where from the 1880s Arthur Smith had plans for an estate in an Italian style to take the place of open fields, although the reality was much less grand.

MISS SCOTT'S MEMORIAL HOME OF REST. Belmont Street, early 1900s. This was one of many such homes which appeared in Bognor in the latter part of the nineteenth century. It was built in 1880.

THE HIGH STREET, c. 1910. Up to the 1790s this was a quiet road, used mainly by local fishermen. Now it is a busy thoroughfare, with the description of 'a very pretty street' applied in the early part of this century, much less applicable. The gardens which once graced one side of the street, now seem part of a completely different world.

THE HIGH STREET. Possibly an even earlier picture, looking in the opposite direction. Someone has drawn attention to the post office (with the clock) on the corner. The traffic did not even run to a lone cyclist on this occasion.

34

THE ARCADE in the High Street, *c*. 1910. Every seaside town should have one and this was Bognor's Arcade, built in 1901/2 by William Nathaniel Tate, local builder, utilising the gardens of York House. It was actually intended as an approach to The Theatre Royal. It remained in the family until sold by his daughter in 1962.

THE ARCADE INTERIOR. Decorated for Christmas in 1905, as it was each year. The ornate entrance at the High Street end used to run to a gold-braided commissionaire, who stood at the ready, to open carriage doors and assist elegant ladies to alight. Each Christmas he dressed as Santa Claus.

THE HIGH STREET 'BY NIGHT', *c.* 1906. This shows the post office and arcade and is relatively busy considering it is intended to show the street at night time. The postcard has had the shop windows, street lamp and a crescent moon, all cut out so that when it is held to the light, they appear lit up. A not uncommon postcard novelty at this period.

ALDWICK ROAD, *c.* 1909. This was the main route to Aldwick, which was becoming a fashionable place to live. The Duff Coopers lived there from the 1920s to the 1930s. Their big cream car must have been a familiar sight along this road, as they patronised local shops. The photographer appears to have had problems with the bright sunlight on the day he took this picture.

WATERLOO SQUARE, *c.* 1903. Open ground originally known as Hothamton Field and intended by Richard Hotham to provide an uninterrupted view of the sea. On the western side, numbers 7 to 17 were built by Daniel Wonham in around 1820 and let as lodgings to visitors. Waterloo House was built by Daniel's son William for his brother Richard, a linen draper. Later still it became the 'Toy Bazaar' owned by the Burgess family and patronised by Queen Mary in 1929. The cart in this picture was owned by Charles John West, a fishmonger and fruiterer, who had premises in the High Street.

BOGNOR LIBRARY, WATERLOO SQUARE. An end of the nineteenth-century photograph of Bognor's famous library and bazaar. What treasures it must have held at that time - it even claimed to have pianofortes for sale.

WATERLOO SQUARE, *c.* 1922. At this time the centre of the square was merely a patch of grazing land on which sheep and cattle were kept before slaughter. A ewe was kept as a decoy to lead sheep out of the field to the slaughter house which was in Norfolk Street (or 'Blood Alley' as the young tearaways called it).

WATERLOO SQUARE. In the early 1930s when the grazing land had gone and gardens had been laid out for enjoyment by the visitors.

WATERLOO SQUARE. A much more modern view, *c*. 1940, showing the gardens and bowling greens. In the 1920s, the Square had been bought by the local council from the Merchant Taylor's Company and the gardens date from that period.

SITTING ROOM, REST LODGE, early 1900s. A typical scene in a seaside rest home of this period. The postcard had been purchased from Burgess's Bazaar.

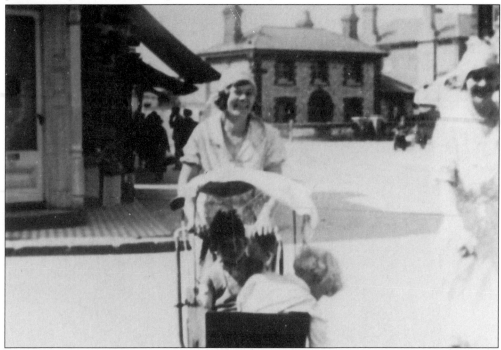

LONDON ROAD, BEDFORD STREET END, 1930s. This is one of the street photographer's pictures so popular at this period in seaside towns. The photographs were taken in an instant and you were handed a slip of paper to take to a shop or booth by teatime to obtain copies. The Sussex flint building in the background is the old police station. The child grabbing the wheel is now the gentleman who kindly lent me the photograph and the two ladies are his aunts.

THE PAVILION, 1920s. This building started life as one of Mr Thompson's seaplane assembly hangers at Middleton in the 1914/18 war. It was purchased by the Council for about £17,000 and erected north of Waterloo Square as a 'Winter Garden', in 1922. It held an audience of 3,000 and the first show was provided by the Co-optimists Concert Party. The first reaction of the townsfolk was less than enthusiastic and there were plenty of jibes about the lath and plastic facade. Its life as an entertainment centre came to an abrupt end in 1948 with a fire. It was closed and dismantled in 1950.

PRINCESS ELIZABETH BOATING POOL AND PAVILION GARDENS, 1930s. The message on the back of the postcard says: 'The pool is formed like a map with different places stamped all round'. It was actually shaped as an outline of England and Wales and was opened on 12 April 1937. (The sender has marked The Methodist Church with a cross).

41

ILLUMINATED GARDENS, BOGNOR REGIS

ILLUMINATED GARDENS, 1930s. Like many other seaside towns, Bognor lit up its gardens at night during the Summer season. One of the minor thrills of my visits to Bognor in the late 1930s was being allowed to walk with my Aunt and cousin back to Rose Green, near Aldwick, after dark through the illuminated gardens.

THE BLACK MILL, NYEWOOD LANE, early 1900s. The mill was built in the 1820s, was derelict by 1900 and demolished soon after. It was used for making cement for facing many Bognor houses, although in 1880 it had been used for grinding flour. Henry Martin who had a mill for grinding chalk at Littlehampton was the original owner. In mid-Victorian days it was operated by William Attfield, who sold his cement in nine shilling barrels. Nearby was the Mill Field where horse races were held in the 1840s and 60s and where local tradesmen had stalls.

UPPER BOGNOR ROAD, c. 1905. This road, which was a continuation of the High Street, has always been considered one of the most pleasant areas of Bognor - although the rustic seat wouldn't stand much chance with today's traffic. It had many fine houses amongst the shady trees and often appeared on picture postcards in the early 1900s.

UPPER BOGNOR ROAD, c. 1913. Guide books of this period usually singled out this part of Bognor for praise, dwelling on the nearby park grounds and the many fine trees. One of the lads in this picture is equipped with a bucket and spade, so is probably returning from the beach.

Upper Bognor Road.

UPPER BOGNOR ROAD, early 1900s. A beautifully posed picture of this leafy road during the years when young ladies in long white dresses could pause for a rest beside a main road devoid of any sort of pavement; and without any kind of vehicle in sight.

HOTHAM PARK, BOGNOR REGIS

HOTHAM PARK, 1940s. The house and grounds adjacent to the Upper Bognor Road were part of the Aldwick Manor Estate and were purchased by the town council in 1946 for £40,000. The official opening was on 23 May 1947, after much heartsearching as to the most suitable name for the amenity. Regis Park and Hotham Woodlands were both suggested, but the final decision was the more obvious one of Hotham Park - the first time the man responsible for so much of Bognor had been publicly commemorated. The park eventually included a zoo, miniature railway, a cafe, a bandstand, tennis and putting greens and a boating lake - most of which continue to this day.

Three
Fun and Games

TRIUMPHAL ARCH IN LONDON ROAD. This was to celebrate Queen Victoria's Diamond Jubilee in 1897. Presumably, many of the townsfolk in the picture had a hand in building the arch - and don't they look pleased with themselves, including even the dog.

TRIUMPHAL ARCH in July 1900, for the opening of the Princess Mary Homes by the Duke and Duchess of York (see also page 27).

HIGH STREET, 4 April 1906. Triumphal arches had become quite a tradition in Bognor. This was for a Royal Visit to the town. There was also to be another for King George V's Coronation in 1910.

GAME OF CROQUET taking place on the lawn between Glamis Street and Church Path (to the left). The picture is undated, but the clothes point to the early 1900s. 'The Laurels', a flint cottage in Church Path was reputed to have housed a ghost, a white figure standing near a piano. There was also the sound of organ music and doors opening and closing where none existed.

BOAT CART ON BOGNOR BEACH, c. 1923. A very ususual mode of transport operated by Leonard Lee. The boy at the back of the cart is wearing the very popular sailor suit. The photographer has been unfair to the horse, having neatly beheaded it.

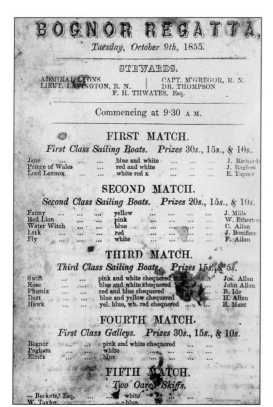

PROGRAMME OF BOGNOR REGATTA, Tuesday 9 October 1855. This included ladies and gents races, a greasy pole contest, a mock sea battle and an old fishing boat to be set alight. This was October, although August seems to have been the more usual month for the annual event. On Regatta Day in August 1896, 2,500 people passed through the pier turnstiles.

'SHAMROCK', the winner of Bognor Regatta, although unfortunately the year is not known. Included in this fine picture are Basie (?) Ragless, Joe Ragless and Tom Mant. Ragless was, of course, a very historic and enduring name in Bognor fishing circles.

FETE IN AID OF THE R.C. CHURCH, early 1920s. This was at The Den just off the High Street and the lady in the centre is Mrs Grisewood. It is not clear whether the umbrellas are because of rain, or sun. The Den (originally Sudley cottage) was built in 1827/30 and later enlarged in the 1860s by Claude Bowes-Lyon (great-grandfather of Queen Elizabeth II), who nicknamed the building, 'The Lyon's Den'. It was struck by a bomb in the last war and was afterwards demolished. The name persists in Den Avenue.

GROUP FROM BOGNOR REGIS GYMNASTIC CLUB at Rose Green in July 1936. Mrs M.E. Tippen provided this photograph and her late husband is included. His mother was also a member of the club and on her retirement she was presented with an inscribed clock, which is now owned by her daughter-in-law.

THE PICTUREDOME, Bognor's distinctive cinema shown here in the 1920s. It was built originally as The New Assembly Rooms, although even in 1886 it was showing magic-lantern type films. Just after the First World War it was converted into a cinema, showing silent films. The first programme on 5 June 1919 included the film *Boundary House* and another of that year's Derby.

PROGRAMME OF SILENT FILMS at Bognor Pier Pavilion, at the sea end of pier, 1909. Films were shown here from 1909/12 and after this a full size cinema was built over the pier entrance. Films included such titles as *The Ragpicker's Daughter*, *Making Charcoal*, and *Tyler's Topical Slides of the Week's Doings*. The accompanist was Miss May Pettitt L.A.M.

THE INFIRMARY PARADE, 1911. These were held annually in aid of the local hospital. Notice the float entitled 'Caught on Bognor Rocks'. What kind of creature was this, we wonder. A housemaid in her distinctive uniform has stepped out to see the parade in the foreground. Note also the word FIRE on the lamp post.

BOGNOR VOLUNTEER FIRE BRIGADE in all their glory in a parade early this century. Captain Edward Wood is in the foreground. The Brigade had been born at a meeting in 1873 and a purpose-built fire station was erected in the High Street in 1899. Horses had to be borrowed for calls and the men were told 'save your horses as much as possible, do not gallop them uphill. Do not hesitate to make the crew dismount'.

FLOAT IN PARADE. Possibly the Peace Celebrations procession on 19 July 1919. This is the first of two mystery photographs.

RALLY AT RAILWAY STATION. Even more of a mystery than the last picture. No date (although obviously after 1902 when the station was built). The Fire Brigade are present, as are dignitaries in an expensive car and a fair-sized crowd. Can any reader help?

FELPHAM HARVEST HOME, 1868. A very early picture of what was almost certainly an annual event at that time. The Harvest Homes (or Suppers) were provided for the farm workers by the farmers or big landowners and were usually held in the largest barn available, although in this case marquees are being used. Often men only would be invited (with perhaps a separate supper arranged for the women and children), but this appears to be a thoroughly mixed gathering. Sometimes the children would become involved, when the proceedings would take on a more sedate character.

SHOPWHYKE BEADLES AT WALBERTON. Undated photograph, but possibly 1920s. A common country sight, but with the addition of a well-dressed lady with an imposing hat. Shopwhyke is a hamlet near Oving.

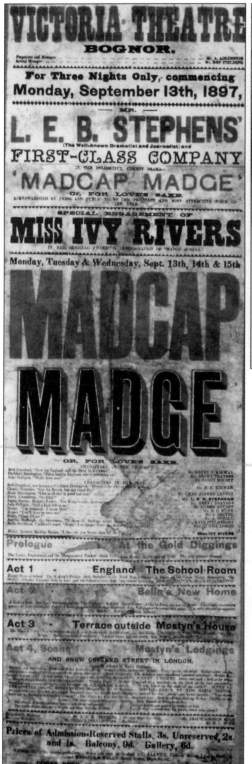

PAINTING OF H.G. PELISSIER by John Collier, on a poster for the Pier Theatre. We have the date, 13 September, but unfortunately no year.

VICTORIA THEATRE PLAY POSTER, 13 September 1897. A three night stand of a comedy drama *Madcap Madge* or *For Love's Sake* with the special engagement of Miss Ivy Rivers and starring Mr L.E.B. Stephens. Prices ranged from sixpence to three shillings. This was the second performance at the theatre, the first being *Over the Indian Frontier*. Originally the theatre had been a non-conformist chapel and not surprisingly there was some prejudice in the town at a former place of worship becoming a place of entertainment.

TIPPER'S BAND, 7 September 1906. A popular Bognor band at this time. They often played in the Western Bandstand, which is where they are posed for their picture by a well-known Bognor photographer, Mr W. P. Marsh.

BOGNOR POST OFFICE MINSTRELS, 1905. In this picture, probably in The Victoria Theatre, London Road, is Thomas Wood, the Post Office Overseer.

WALTER HOWARD AND HIS JOLLITY BOYS. A very popular group of seaside entertainers photographed on the Western Parade beach. Walter was a banjo player and his group included Ben Walters, who had worked for Fred Karno, and Tom Sheridan, a baritone from the Carl Rosa Opera. They dressed in red blazers and white trousers and came down from London to Bognor each May for the summer season. They would often begin with a show in the forecourt of an inn in the High Street and then establish their pitch at the end of Nyewood Lane. Their stage had a dressing room at the rear and their show was said to be slicker than the one presented by Uncle George Edgar, on his pitch near the Steyne. Sometimes their rivalry made the council shift them further apart.

WALTER HOWARD'S GAY CADETS, *c.* 1913. By this time Walter Howard had renamed his group, perhaps feeling that The Gay Cadets sounded a little more impressive than The Jollity Boys. Here they are on their portable stage, with presumably several of their patrons. The message on the reverse says: 'This is the only postcard with any of us in, so am sending it.'

WALTER HOWARD'S GAY CADETS ON THE WESTERN PARADE, *c.* 1914. This gives a good idea of the size of the stage and how the audience sat on deck chairs on the beach, or watched from the prom above. The gentleman in the white suit is apparently 'the bottler' attempting to extract contributions from the spectators. This seems a precarious way of making a living, although they performed on the beach three times daily and Walter Howard was said to have often entertained the Royal Family at Sandringham.

UNCLE GEORGE'S CONCERT PARTY, on the beach in the early 1900s. Uncle George Edgar, real name Augustus Sears, played seven seasons at Margate before settling in Bognor. His group were known as The Thespians and were very popular with the children, providing them with a song and dance competition each week. Noel Coward was said to have won a prize one week in 1904. Much later The Thespians were included in Noel Coward's 'Cavalcade' but this was after Uncle George's death.

UNCLE GEORGE AS A SOLO ACT, *c.* 1922 (his 28th season). By this time he had given up the group and was entertaining with a portable harmonium on the East side of Waterloo Square. He had enchanted the Bognor holidaymakers, especially the children, since 1897, and died in 1928.

FRANK BALE AND HIS LIVING MARIONETTES, c. 1922. Mr Bale was known affectionately as 'Bognor's Clown' and performed on the beach three times daily in the 1920s. The Marionettes had live heads on puppet's bodies and were remarkably effective. He paid £1 a year to rent his pitch.

FRANK BALE, 'THE BOGNOR CLOWN'. He performed with his daughter, Miss Vi, and his dog Tozer. As well as operating the marionettes, he also played the banjo and guitar and was a juggler and a clown. It must have been a wearing lifestyle, with shows at 11 am, 3 pm and 6 pm. This picture shows the tiny booth from which he presented his 'Playtime'.

FANCY DRESS PARTY, TANGMERE. These were the ladies of the Women's Royal Air Force enjoying themselves off duty, probably just after the First World War. The Curator of the Tangmere Air Museum tells me that this is a fairly commonly seen photograph, although he is unable to date it more precisely. The WRAFs became the WAAFs at the beginning of the Second World War in 1939. Perhaps a reader can provide more information.

'SISTERS DELPHINE'. No date or information about this, except that the photograph is by King and Wilson, Theatrical Photographers, 8 Pier Arcade, Bognor. So probably they appeared at the Pier Theatre.

Four
Churches, Chapels and Schools

SOUTH BERSTED VICARAGE GARDEN PARTY. Church Lane, early 1900s. There is a splendid array of headgear and the spire of the church, which owed much to Sir Richard Hothman, can be seen peeping above the trees. An account early in the previous century said that: 'The Vicarage garden and orchard are tasteful and pleasant - a little retreat wholly screened from the public eye'. The Bersted Band (known as Dicky Sharpe's Hogweed Band) is in attendance at the rear. Genteel merrymaking of this sort was wholly at variance with the Bognor Fairs held every July in the eighteenth, and up to the early nineteenth, century. These were very irritating to the gentry and were described as 'exciting for the young and giddy, with a strong tendency to harm' and were said to be full of 'gaping spectators and noisy buffoons'. Included were freak shows, beer tents, boxing booths and of course, the Sussex favourite - Gingerbread.

OLD ST JOHN'S CHAPEL TOWER, early 1900s. This was in The Steyne, the tower with the clock and bell named Mary Anne having been added to the chapel in 1833. The Revd Edward Miller, first Vicar of Bognor, reigned here from 1838. He loved long sermons, some of which he repeated annually. When the children misbehaved during his orations, he dealt out summary punishment on the spot with a cane he kept handy. In 1891 the chapel was pulled down, leaving only the clock tower as a landmark.

ST JOHN'S CHURCH, London Road. A flint and brick building, opened in 1882, with the spire added in 1895. The delay in adding the spire sparked off rumours that the tower of the church was unsafe. These were completely unfounded, but they just added to a strange popular belief that there was a curse on the Vicars of Bognor. The church was demolished and replaced by shops (Boots and W.H.Smith) in 1975.

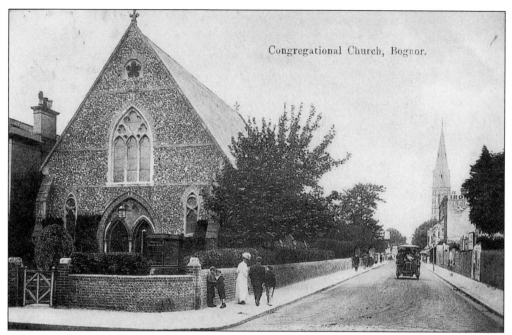

Congregational Church, Bognor.

THE CONGREGATIONAL CHURCH, *c.* 1910. This was built in 1869 on the corner of London Road, making use of local flints, at a cost of £2,620. The site was sold in 1929 and a new church built in Linden Road in 1930. St John's Church can also be seen at the further end of the road.

Bognor Congregational
S.S. Treat to ARUNDEL. JULY, 1927

CONGREGATIONAL SUNDAY SCHOOL TREAT TO ARUNDEL, July 1927. This was very typical of these annual treats organised by local churches to keep their younger members loyal. One of the youngsters in the front row was unable to restrain herself and failed to heed the photographer's injunction to 'keep absolutely still'.

ROMAN CATHOLIC CHURCH, 'OUR LADY OF SEVEN DOLOURS', Clarence Road. The church was designed for the Servite Order by Joseph Hansom, son of the man who designed Arundel's R.C. Cathedral. It was opened on 16 August 1882. Earlier Bognor Roman Catholics had walked to masses in Slindon or Chichester, at least until a small chapel was opened in a room above a grocer's shop in Steyne Street. When the Servites arrived in Bognor, the feeling against them led almost to 'No Popery' riots.

High Altar, R.C. Church, Bognor

HIGH ALTAR, ROMAN CATHOLIC CHURCH. The Servite Order who provided priests for this church, had been founded in Italy in the thirteenth century by seven rich men. They came to London in the latter part of the nineteenth century and established a church in Fulham Road, dedicated to the sufferings of the Holy Mother, with many beautiful ceremonies, which were also carried out in the Bognor church.

ST PHILIP'S ALTAR, ROMAN CATHOLIC CHURCH. This was the altar dedicated to St Philip Benizi, an important figure in the history of the Servite Order. In thirteenth-century Italy he became first a lay brother and later general of the Order. His popularity was such that he had to hide to avoid being made Pope. He died in 1285.

ST WILFRID'S CHURCH, VICTORIA DRIVE. This was opened in 1910 and this picture probably dates from soon after this time. When St John's Church in London Road was demolished and its site sold, the status of Parish Church of Bognor passed to St Wilfrid's. Someone has written on the back of the picture, 'An outnumbered cow'. This must surely give an idea of how rural Bognor had remained even up to the early years of this century.

65

THE MERCHANT TAYLOR'S HOME CHAPEL, *c.* 1930s. The home closed in 1954, eventually to be demolished. The chapel in the grounds survived for a few more years until 1959 (see page 32).

WALBERTON SCHOOL CHILDREN AND SCHOOL, *c.* 1937. The pupils are enjoying milk from Mr Cox's Dairy in Slindon, in the days when primary school children were given a third of a pint of milk at school daily. The first school in the village was opened in 1874, with an endowment of £12 annually from a bequest of John Nash in 1732. In past centuries, Walberton children carried Garlands each May Day. In 1851 one little girl lost all but a halfpenny out of the fourpence she had collected, when her father confiscated the larger share to spend on his 'bakker'.

NORTH BERSTED CHURCH SCHOOL. Mr Bowden and his gardening class. No date, but almost certainly early in this century. Many schools had such classes, which were popular and practical. In the picture are some boys in what appear to be the uniform of the Boys Brigade.

EVERSLEY SCHOOL FOR GIRLS, 1920s. A school play being performed in the open, probably in 1927. The school was in Colebrook Terrace, in a large house next to a boys school. By 1911 it was referred to as The Church of England High School, preparing girls for the teaching and other professions. The building was demolished in 1947.

ST MARY'S CHURCH, FELPHAM, c. 1906. This is a medieval church, which suffered like so many from nineteenth-century restoration. The tower was added at the end of the fifteenth century. The Tower Clock commemorated Queen Victoria's Golden Jubilee. The church entrance is set off by the fine lych gate, which was erected in 1897 - this time commemorating the Queen's Diamond Jubilee.

ST MARY'S CHURCH, YAPTON, early 1900s. The church dates from 1180/1220, and as Nairn and Pevsner say in *The Buildings of England* (1965), it is worth a special visit, as so much of the early centuries have survived. On the north side a very old yew tree was used to provide branches for Palm Sunday. Several crosses can be seen on parts of the church, which it is believed were made by pilgrims on their way to the shrine of St Richard at Chichester. The rhyme here says, 'Shut the gate and clap'n. Say the bells of Yapton'.

Five
Trade and Transport

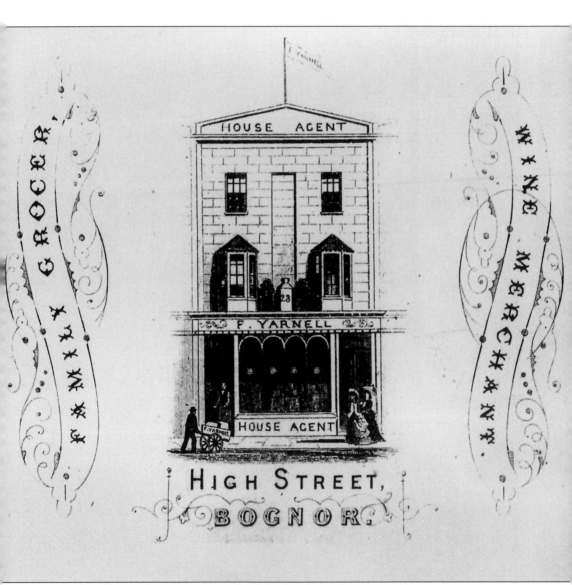

TRADE CARD OF FREDERICK YARNELL, family grocer, wine merchant and house agent at 23 High Street. The card is undated but it must have been pre-1900. His Telegraphic Address in 1886 was 'Ozone, Bognor'. The very attractive card has all the feel of a highly successful Victorian business.

CHENEY'S BUTCHER'S SHOP, Station Road, Christmas 1925. In the picture, Ernie Cheney, Frank Earley (the manager) and Fred Booker. The shop sold its own Southdown lamb. It was taken over by Parfrements in 1970.

L. Field's Butcher's Shop. A picture that looks far back into the last century. A Directory of 1903 mentions Mrs Louisa Ann Field, Butcher of West Street. The display of meat would make any late twentieth-century food inspector shudder.

MILK FLOAT OF WOODBINE DAIRY, early 1900s. The dairy was owned by the Misses Fanny and Emily Robinson, florists, of Woodbine Cottage, Upper Bognor Road, but was run by the Humphrey family. Fred Humphrey is seen here on the float. These nippy little carts were a familiar sight on the roads in the early part of this century. From the big churn, milk was dispensed to the housewives straight into their jugs. The horses knew all the regular calls, without being told where to stop.

FREDERICK SMITH, BAKER AND CONFECTIONER, 43 London Road, c. 1910. Fred was a noted maker of pork pies (and also a beer retailer) at these premises, carrying on the trade founded by his father (also Frederick) in a shop in Market Street. The pie making was continued by Smith Junior's widow in London Road, until 1929. Frederick Smith senior was reputed to have invented the raised pork pie in 1868.

REYNOLD'S STEAM VAN, early 1900s. The locally famous firm of Reynolds and Co., house furnishers, was established in 1867 and is still going strong.

BRICKYARD, Collyer Avenue area. Early 1900s. This was owned by the Geall family who were well-known local brickmakers and builders from the 1890s. They had brickworks in North and South Bersted and in Pagham.

BRICKMAKERS, Collyer Avenue area, early 1900s. Sir Richard Hotham had his own brickyard and boasted that his bricks were better than those of the Duke of Richmond. After his death in 1799, work came to an end, until expansion really took off in the late nineteenth century. Wood moulds were used to shape the bricks which were then laid in rows to be wind-dried. When dry they were built into a stack, or clamp, which could contain as many as 100,000 bricks. The clamp was covered with clay and fired with coal, burning for six to eight weeks. Meanwhile, it had to be watched night and day in case the fires went out.

FISHERMEN AND THEIR POTS, turn of the century. Bognor was only a fishing village until the late eighteenth century, but in spite of having no harbour, fishing was very good, especially for crabs and lobsters - particularly off the famed Bognor Rocks. Traditionally, there were seven good things from Sussex, including a Selsey Cockle and a Chichester Lobster. The latter were caught off Bognor and Selsey, sometimes as many as four or five in one pot.

BOGNOR FISHERMEN, 1920s. This photograph was taken to commemorate a very big catch of herrings from one of the many small boats which came ashore filled to capacity at this time. It was considered to be one of the biggest local catches for years.

MAKING PRAWN POTS, early 1900s. A guidebook of the nineteenth century said, 'Bognor is celebrated for prawns, lobsters, oysters and silver mullet. Great quantities are sent to the London Market. The visitor is advised to order fish a day beforehand, or send to market early in the morning'.

Felpham Beach near Bognor
Published by R. Briant Burgess, Bognor

FISHERMEN ON FELPHAM BEACH, early this century. The withes to make the traps in which the lobsters, crabs and prawns were taken, were cut around Christmas, and bought from farmers. To preserve the pots they were dipped in tar, to make them last about two years. In shape they resembled the old-fashioned straw beehives. Large flints provided the weight to carry the pots to the bottom. The prawn pots were sunk at night and baited with pieces of fish.

75

BOGNOR URBAN DISTRICT COUNCIL DUSTCART, c. 1900. The Urban District Council was formed in 1894, carrying on from a Local Government Board of 1867. In the early nineteenth century, Bognor had a dustman or scavenger, who plied his trade with a horse and cart.

CORN HARVEST, c. 1908. It must not be forgotten that as well as the sea, Bognor was also dependent on the land for much of its rural economy. Mr T.W. Money bought a dairy in Station Road, in 1909. The cows were milked at the rear of the shop, with an entrance by a lane from Crescent Road and they grazed the meadows where Longfield Road is now. Mr Money bought Manor Farm, North Bersted in 1914 and most of the farm still belongs to the family. When King George V was convalescing at Craigweil House in 1929, milk from a Jersey cow called 'Mouse' at Manor Farm was sent for his use each day. The picture from Mr R. Money, is of the harvest in Berry Field, which is to the west of Manor Farm. In the foreground are Bill Wingate and Bill Keates.

SEAPLANE AT ANCHOR, 3 August 1912. This was Claude Grahame-White in his Henry Farman plane, pausing at Bognor on a round trip sponsored by *The Daily Mail*.

FIRST PLANE TO LAND ON BOGNOR BEACH, 26 May 1913. The first plane seen over Bognor was a biplane piloted by Douglas Graham Gilmore on 8 May 1911; but this was said to be the first to actually land. The pilot was called Cecil Pashley, later to be chief flying instructor at Shoreham. The occasion was an air display, which included 5 minute trips at a cost of 2 guineas.

COACHES LEAVING FOR GOODWOOD FROM ROYAL PIER HOTEL, *c.* 1911. Goodwood fortnight was always an important time for Bognor, with many people staying in the town and making use of the coaches provided from the big hotels. This is the Royal Pier Hotel, which later changed its name to The Royal. They claimed to have the choicest wines in the town.

COACH TAKING VISITORS FROM THE NORFOLK, *c.* 1913. Their destination would have been either Goodwood Races, or perhaps just a country run. On the box is Mr Mearman. Standing are Sid Webber and at the horse's head is Ned Morris, with Henry Warren. On the balcony is Walter Stride.

HORSE BUS, 1860s. From an advertisement in a Bognor guide, showing the Norfolk Hotel, before it became 'Royal'.

BOGNOR POSTMEN IN SNOW, 30 December 1908. They are standing outside the main post office in what was a very severe winter. *The Evening Argus* said the snow fell so heavily in Sussex that those who hankered after an old-fashioned Christmas will have had more than enough to satisfy them. On 28 December a train was stranded in Clayton Tunnel near Brighton and the tram service was suspended, bringing all business to a standstill.

BRIGANTINE WRECKED ON BOGNOR BEACH, 1880s. Coal was often delivered from boats of this kind directly on to the beach, but this one came to grief. The local photographer Mr W.P. Marsh was soon on the scene to preserve the disaster for posterity.

CYCLE AND CAR ON BOGNOR SANDS, Easter Saturday, April 1914. The smooth sands were very useful for events such as this. Were they racing, I wonder?

THE SILVER QUEEN' BUS, 1920s. At the end of the First World War, Mr Cecil Walling
purchased a converted field ambulance and used it for passengers from Slindon into Bognor.
This proved so popular that he acquired a real single decker bus, which became his first 'Silver
Queen'. Later he acquired two more buses and could then operate an hourly service to Bognor
and a Wednesday service to Chichester. The Silver Queens were viewed with affection, as the
drivers would stop anywhere and would collect parcels and shopping. The last bus from
Walberton carried a post box, which was much used as it meant that letters caught the last
collection in Bognor. In 1944, Mr Walling retired and was presented with a pewter mug and an
illuminated address. The little bus service had a slogan, 'Never anyone left behind.'

RED ROVER BUS, *c.* 1925. This tiny bus garage was at Felpham. The bus was typical of the little vehicles which operated on rural routes in the early years of this century. This one linked Felpham, Pagham, Aldwick and Bognor.

BOGNOR RAIL STATION AFTER FIRE, 29 September 1899. Bognor's first station had previously collapsed in a gale and had the platform roof blown off in a storm. In the fire, the wooden platform was completely destroyed. The suggested cause - a porter's coat left to dry in front of a fire.

BOGNOR RAILWAY STATION, early 1900s. This handsome brick-built station was built in July 1902, one of the first constructed in this way in the whole country. W. Johnson and Co. were the builders and the cost was £37,000. It contained a large booking hall, parcels office, refreshment rooms and accommodation for the station master.

ANOTHER VIEW OF THE RAILWAY STATION. This shows the imposing clock tower which graced the main building. During the building of the new station, old goods wagons were used as makeshift offices and passengers and staff suffered a fair amount of inconvenience, but this was considered well worthwhile when the new building was completed.

INTERIOR OF RAILWAY STATION, 1905. The concourse contained a book stall and fruit stall, as well as a cabin for the use of taxi cab drivers. The obligitory weighing machine can be seen on the left. Bognor in 1846 had to be content with a small halt, three-and-a-half miles north of the town. It was named Bognor station, but was in fact in the middle of fields and the only way to get to the town was by walking, or by the use of Edwin Newman's horse bus. In 1852 it was more sensibly renamed 'Woodgate - for Bognor'. Eventually, in 1864, Bognor had its own branch line and its very own station and Woodgate station was closed later that year.

GYPSYHILL LOCOMOTIVE AT BOGNOR, *c.* 1900s. This was a Stroudley A Class Terrier, built in June 1877. An advertisement for Charles Knowles can be seen on the right. He was a cabinet maker, furniture remover, house agent and funeral furnisher, with premises in Station Road.

BOGNOR STATION STAFF, about 1902/10. How smart they looked, with the station master George Henry Gilham in the middle. Not all the staff were in this photograph, as others had to keep the station going.

MINIATURE RAILWAY, early 1900s. Called on this card rather misleadingly 'a model railway', it was on the site of the Kursaal. The locomotive was made in Harpenden by Mr Robert Briggs and weighed about half a ton.

THE CHILDREN'S RAILWAY again, showing the type of carriages in use. Another Bognor miniature railway later ran from 1948 to 1952 on the land now occupied by Butlin's Holiday Camp. There was also a miniature railway on the pier in the 1950s and 60s. Notice the advertisement in this photograph for Freeman, Hardy and Willis.

Six
Popular Personalities

MARY WHEATLAND, or 'Our Mary' as she was often known. She was Bognor's most famous Bathing Woman for 62 years. She saved 30 lives and was awarded 2 medals and 2 certificates. She died aged 89 in 1924. This lovely studio photograph was taken by W.P. Marsh, who described himself as Artist Photographer, with the Bognor School of Photography at Waterloo Square.

A Bognor Celebrity
Mary Wheatland who has saved over 60 lives.

MARY WHEATLAND when an old lady. She was born in 1835 and began her career at 14, hiring out bathing costumes, giving swimming lessons and looking after the cumbersome bathing machines which were then in vogue. Her machines were recognised by being painted with red and yellow stripes. She claimed that no bather had ever drowned on her beach. Her party piece was to stand with her head in the water, waving her button boots in the air.

THE BOGNOR BATHING WOMEN.
MARY WHEATLAND AND DAUGHTER.

MARY WHEATLAND AND HER DAUGHTER. Mary was recognised as a local 'character' and many stories and legends grew up around her. She was always seen in a long rough serge dress and a sailor type hat with her name on it. She retired at 74, finding diving off the end of Bognor pier just a bit too much. Her daughter (also Mary) carried on her work.

BOGNOR'S MERMAID.

WOMAN OF 72 WHO HAS SAVED 30 LIVES.

A little old woman stands on the parade at Bognor looking out to sea. She is clad in a rough blue serge costume, on the bodice of which two life-saving medals are pinned. A battered sailor hat, bearing her name in gold letters, is tied under her chin with black ribbons. The weather-beaten face is crumpled up into a net-work of smiles.

She is Mary Wheatman, the bathing woman at Bognor, and she smiles because she is quite young still—only seventy-two! Fifty-eight years ago Mary first went to Bognor, a slip of a girl, aged fourteen, and there she has remained as bathing attendant to this day.

An "Express" representative went down to visit Mary Wheatman yesterday, and was taken into her neat bathing hut, on the walls of which are proudly displayed two testimonials from the Royal Humane Society.

"How many lives have I saved?" Mary replied to the first query. "Only about thirty, as far as I can remember. I did not start life-saving at once. Fourteen seemed a bit too young; but three months before my sixteenth birthday I went out to sea and brought in a Mrs. Woods who had got out of her depth.

Mary has some admiration for the bathing customs of 1860 as compared with those of the present time.

"There were none of those pretty bathing gowns in those days," she said, scornfully, adding, with a twinkle in her eyes, "but then there was no mixed bathing. Ladies' costumes were made of stout blue serge, shaped like a sack, and tied round the waist. There were no bathing caps, because people did not mind their hair coming out of curl."

Mary gave up diving from the pier on her seventy-first birthday. She thought she was getting rather too old for that, but she dives off a boat, and thinks nothing of swimming to the pier-head and back, a distance of half a mile.

NEWSPAPER REPORT ON BOGNOR'S MERMAID. Not many people are famous enough to have a newspaper cutting on them reproduced as a postcard. Unfortunately although the story reads well, they managed to get her name wrong, calling her Mary Wheatman, rather than Wheatland.

MARY WHEATLAND'S FUNERAL. Mary died aged 89 in 1924 and here is her funeral procession leaving Ivy Lane in April of that year. She was sincerely mourned by a great many of her fellow townsfolk, who felt that Bognor would never be quite the same without the 'Grace Darling of the South Coast'.

NORTH BERSTED POLICE STATION, 1902. The policeman is P.C. Dubbings. In 1843 Bognor had 'The Cage', a combined prison and police station in a yard in Bedford Street, off the High Street. The first police station proper was in Dorset Gardens in 1867.

THE FIRST UNIFORMED POSTMAN IN BOGNOR. Sadly, the picture is undated. the first post office at the turn of the century was in Derby House in the High Street and this was followed by several others in the same vicinity. William Hayley the poet had troubles with his post in 1811, claiming that the postman carried his letters around in his pocket, instead of delivering them promptly. He said that he was put to great inconvenience when his proofs were so late that he scarcely had time to revise them.

H.M. KING GEORGE V AND QUEEN MARY at Craigwell House, April 1929. Much to many people's surprise it was announced on 22 January 1929 that the fragile King would recuperate at Aldwick, near Bognor, and here he remained for almost 13 weeks. His alleged words when later he was asked if he would like to return, seem to be a favourite quote whenever Bognor is mentioned in casual conversation. It has often been stated that he did not utter the words at all, or that he said something similar, but much more polite. Probably we shall never know and I am content to leave it at that.

GEORGE V AND QUEEN MARY seen here with the little Princess - now our present Queen. It is on record that she enjoyed building sand castles, just as so many of her subjects had done before and since.

QUEEN MARY SHOPPING in April 1929, in Burgess' Bazaar, on the S.W. corner of Waterloo Square. The large crowds show the popularity of the Queen.

KING GEORGE V AND QUEEN MARY. The King's first public appearance since his illness, on Saturday 30 March 1929. The King sat on the lawn to hear a concert by the Kneller Band playing by royal command. He was watched by a crowd from the beach. He returned to Windsor on 15 May 1929. The town was to be rewarded a few weeks later when it was announced that royal approval to add the word Regis to the town's name had been granted.

OLD PAGHAM RESIDENTS, *c.* 1905. A lovely camera study of an old gentleman with his clay pipe. Unfortunately, we do not know his name or anything about him, although quite possibly he came from the fishing community.

A similar photograph to the last, with the subject even more likely to be a fisherman. These two old gentlemen probably spent some time in the local pub. From one of these hostelries a few stories survive; for instance, one old shepherd was at supper enjoying his roast lamb. He said with great satisfaction: 'Ah, many a time you said Baa to me. Now I can say Baa to thee'. Another tale: one man said 'Did you know poor Old Harry has had his leg off? The reply was 'What, foot and all?' They drank pints of 'Old', played shove ha'penny and darts and had a spit pot handy on the floor.

OLD BOGNOR FOLK IN GARDEN OF ST JOHN'S IN THE HIGH STREET. Undated photograph, but probably around the early 1900s. They had all benefitted from the 'Bognor Observer Beef Fund'.

OLD AGE PENSIONERS RECEIVING THEIR FIRST FIVE SHILLING HANDOUT. The York Road Post Office, January 1909. On the right: postmaster Edward 'Timber' Wood and on the left: his brother Tom Wood. We do not know the name of the dog. They probably all knew the popular Bognor catch phrase 'Beautiful Dripping'. This circulated in the 1890s, coming originally from an old woman who sold dripping from the Goodwood kitchens. She knocked at Bognor doors, always offering 'Beautiful Dripping'. It became the town's accolade for anything really good.

OLD LADY, early 1900s. She sits in the doorway of her cottage in Mead Lane, later to become Durban Cottage. Her grandchild can be seen in the window. The great fear of old folk at this time was the possibility of ending up in the Workhouse. A prayer used in Workhouses in the Bognor area included the words 'Mercifully grant that being always exercised in good works and daily eating the bread of carefulness, we may use the Liberality of thy Glory and walk worthy of so great benefits, in Sobriety of life, in cheerful Submission to our Governors, in Brotherly Love one towards another and a constant Obedience to the Word.'

MR FRED HELLYER, an old fisherman with his clay pipe, reading *The People* newspaper, 1890s. The title of the study is 'A Quiet Enjoyment'. This is one of a set of photographs of old Bognor fishermen.

REVD GEORGE FORBES WILD, priest, Evangelist and resident Chaplain, at Butlin's Bognor Regis Holiday Camp, 1960s. Not the sort of picture we normally associate with holiday camps, but undoubtedly many people will have good memories of him.

GIBBET ON BOGNOR BEACH. An undated print, perhaps inspired by the smuggling that went on so freely in the area in the eighteenth century. If this gibbet actually existed, it must have been erected as a warning to wrongdoers. It even appears as if a young lad is having the lesson pointed out to him.

Seven

The Stamp House

THE FAMOUS JUBILEE STAMP HOUSE. North Bersted, Bognor in the late nineteenth or early twentieth century. This was a flint built pub on the Chichester Road, opened in 1873 as 'The Rising Sun'. At the time of Queen Victoria's Golden Jubilee, Richard Sharpe the landlord, accepted a wager to paper one room entirely with postage stamps from his collection.

THE STAMP HOUSE. A little later than the preceding picture, as the ivy has now covered up most of the front wall of the building and a large notice 'Ye Olde Stamp House' has been erected. Within a short time of Mr Sharpe's original idea of sticking stamps on the walls of one of his rooms, he was inundated with more stamps and had to add them to the ceiling and the furniture. This took about five years and there were said to be two million stamps employed. Soon the collection spread to other parts of the pub and even to the summerhouse in the garden. In the hallway, one door was said to have been covered with Western Australian stamps, much coveted by collectors.

THE STAMP HOUSE. Another picture, showing the side of the building where Lloyd's News have evidently paid for an advertisement which includes the title Jubilee Stamp House. Richard Sharpe bought stamps by the thousand to carry on his scheme and of course many were donated. The total value must have been considerable - £80,000 was suggested, although this seems unlikely at that time, particulary as it would appear that the stamps must have been damaged in sticking them to the walls and furniture and in threading them into 'serpents' (pause whilst present-day philatelists shudder).

MR RICHARD SHARPE. He seems to have been a man of many parts as well as running his pub and a small grocers shop adjoining, he obviously enjoyed his pets, as this picture shows. There was his huge stamp collection which threatened to take over the whole building and not content with that he ran the Bersted Brass and Reed Band, known affectionately as 'Dickie Sharpe's Hog-Weed Band'.

THE STAMP HOUSE RUSTIC GARDEN. Mr Sharpe is at the door of his Summer House which was also covered inside with stamps, part of the two million that took up so much of the main building. At one period the number who had viewed the stamps was said to be 716,890 although we are not told exactly what period this covered.

THE STAMP HOUSE AND SERPENTS. Many of the stamps were threaded on strings in this fashion and anyone who has tried this will realise just how many stamps it needs to make up just one short snake. Many other curios such as a laquered Eiffel Tower could be viewed in the building.

ROOM IN THE STAMP HOUSE. This is one of the many picture postcards that were sold in the pub and other places in Bognor, during the early years of this century. This one has an inscription handwritten on the back 'About five miles of stamps. Photo taken through the window. About 120 visitors on Monday'.

THE STAMP ROOM. This was where it all started. By 1911, 600,000 signatures were in 24 Visitors Books. I wonder whether Richard ever regretted embarking on such a scheme, which must have grown to take over his life. There was no entrance fee to view the stamps, although a catalogue of the collection was on sale.

ANOTHER VIEW OF THE STAMP ROOM. By the late 1930s, when I was a boy, the Stamp House was still being talked about in Bognor. My Aunt evidently thought it to be still going strong, as she often promised to take me there, although it must have ceased to exist by that time.

A FINAL PICTURE OF THE STAMP ROOM. One more of the many picture postcards produced to sell to visitors. As well as the straightforward covering of walls and the infamous 'Serpents', the stamps were also fashioned into Queen Victoria's likeness, the Royal Coat of Arms and the Prince of Wales' Feathers.

Mr. R. Sharpe, Jubilee Stamp House, North Bersted, near Bognor.

RICHARD SHARPE. *The Bognor Regis Observer* reported on 3 September 1930 that Mr Sharpe had passed away on Tuesday of the previous week (26 August 1930), his eldest son having taken over the license of the pub. It is unclear when it ceased to be a tourist attraction by reason of its stamps, but it is said that when the collection was broken up, the stamps were given to schoolboys. The Rising Sun building was closed and demolished in 1957, being rebuilt in 1987 as a new 'Rising Sun'. Further information to fill the gaps in this account would be welcome.

Eight
The Villages

SOUTH BERSTED. The daily 'rush hour' in the early part of this century. The Bersteds were the original villages of Bognor, a mile from what is now the centre of the town. They were included in the Urban District by 1900. Some of the early thatched cottages remain to enchant the present day tourists. In earlier centuries, when Bognor was full, visitors sometimes took up residence here. The church of St Mary Magdalene with its plain thirteenth-century tower, underwent restoration in 1879/81.

'THE LAST OF THE THATCH', c. 1922. This is how they described this picture of the demolition of South Bersted's inn 'The Prince of Wales'. The building dated from the seventeenth century and was known locally as 'The Bacon Loft', as bacon was smoked in the roof. In the picture, second from the right, is Dan Ede, son of William Ede the landlord from 1892 to 1922.

ALDWICK BEACH, early 1900s. It has always been possible to walk on the beach to Bognor, except at very high tides, but Aldwick folk say they live 6 miles from Chichester, rather than 2 miles from Bognor. This reflects the rivallry which is said to exist between the two places.

ALDWICK DUCK POND, early 1900s. This is a popular local point of reference; such as 'it's half a mile from the Duck Pond'. The signpost looks perilously near the water.

THE DUCK POND CORNER, c. 1912. The picture includes a delightful view of a traditional Sussex wagon. The card was sent by a resident of 'The Scott Memorial Home' in Bognor (see page 33), to Grays in Essex. Ted said, 'You see by this they have sent me to the seaside for a change. I am feeling much better and stronger'. I hope Ted returned home to Essex feeling very refreshed by his seaside break.

FISH LANE, ALDWICK, *c.* 1905. The village rejoices in some beautifully descriptive names for its lanes - Dark Lane (originally called Paradise Lane), Gossamer Lane, Barrack Lane (where once the army held sway), and of course Fish Lane, with its associations with the local fishing community. The residents look to be out for a gentle Sunday afternoon stroll.

ALDWICK VILLAGE, *c.* 1901. My own very happy memories as a boy are of staying with my Aunt in her bungalow at Rose Green, on the edge of Aldwick and of walking into Bognor via the leafy lanes. The Ship Inn in the village is possibly 200 years old. A smuggler's tunnel was said to exist, connecting the inn to the beach. The building was modernised in the 1930s.

ALDWICK OLD PLACE, *c.* 1929. One of Aldwick's many distinguished houses. This part of the Bognor area has long been considered a fashionable place to live.

VILLAGE ROAD, ALDWICK, *c.* 1908. The children stroll unconcernedly in the road, with modern traffic hazards far in the future. But they were on their way, as the writer of the card says, 'Do not bother about my motor cap, as the weather seems improving'. A flint wall, typical of the South Coast is on the left, enclosing the little chapel.

CRAIGWEIL HOUSE, ALDWICK, *c.* 1929. The house was built in the early 1800s and was known then as 'The Pavilion'. It included 30 rooms and sprang into nationwide fame in February 1929 when it was chosen as a convalescent home for King George V (see pages 91 and 92). Its moments of fame over, as it was demolished in 1932.

THE BARN, ALDWICK BAY ESTATE. This was the largest of Aldwick's private estates, once described as 'a miniature Bournemouth'. The old tithe barn (reputedly of sixteenth century origin) was rebuilt in the last century with a traditional musicians gallery. The original name was 'Swingates Barn'. It was the centre of social life on the Estate from 1932 to 1972, suffering a fire in 1954.

ALDWICK BEACH, early 1900s. Popular with children, as the lanes seemed as mysterious as darkest Africa and the beach was seldom crowded. Lady Diane Cooper, who lived in Aldwick, said 'This is where Cornfields give way to Villadom', but early in this century it was still comfortably countryfied.

THE FRENCH BRIG 'CARNOT', 1912. This vessel from Boulogne ran aground on Aldwick Beach on 29 December 1912, a victim of very rough weather. It carried a cargo of 110 barrels of herrings and 160 tonnes of cement. The crew of six, with their dog, managed to struggle ashore and appeared in the village much to the surprise of local people, who were unaware of the mishap. The Littlehampton tug boat *Jumma* was summoned to help refloat *The Carnot*, but was unsuccessful.

ALDWICK BEACH, 1920s. A final look at Aldwick's beach, this time filled with holidaymakers. In spite of the obviously sunny day, many of the adults still refused to dispense with their dark heavy clothes and hats.

FELPHAM, c. 1900. A view across the fields, showing the church of St Mary in the distance. The correct pronunciation - Felpam or Felfam - is still debated. The latter is said to be historically correct, although many locals still appear to prefer the hard 'p' of Felpam.

FELPHAM CHURCH AND CHURCH FARM DAIRY, early 1900s. The local rhyme was 'Come in and welcome, say the church bells of Felpham'. William Blake agreed about its welcome, calling it 'The Sweetest Spot on Earth'.

VICARAGE LANE, FELPHAM, *c.* 1922. The message on this postcard says that the writer liked the village 'Because it's more country than Bognor'. The old Rectory in the lane was said to house a ghost of a Grey Lady, who walked from the building to Hayley's Corner, where she then vanished.

WILLIAM BLAKE'S COTTAGE, *c.* 1927. The visionary and poet William Blake dwelt happily in this cottage for three years, at a time when wheatfields ran down to the sea. His early feelings were 'Away to sweet Felpham, for Heaven is there', but later an incident which involved him in being accused of sedition, marred his Sussex idyll. But whilst he was in Sussex, the atmosphere encouraged his mystical imagination and he had a vision of his dead father and brothers. He also witnessed a 'Fairy Funeral', describing the little folk as being 'The size and colour of green and grey grasshoppers'. It was here he wrote most of his immortal ode, *Jerusalem.*

BLACKSMITH'S GRAVE, early 1900s.
This was the first of the village blacksmiths
buried in the churchyard. William Stone
died in 1808, aged 70 and his wife in 1826.
His blacksmith's forge was two doors from
The George Inn.

BLACKSMITH'S GRAVE, c. 1906. The
second of the Felpham blacksmiths, Edmund
Etherton, died in 1900 aged 72. Both smiths
have the same epitaph, which can be seen
most clearly in this picture. The lines are
often credited to the poet William Hayley,
who lived in the village (certainly he
appeared to enjoy writing epitaphs), but this
is almost certainly incorrect, as similar lines
appear on gravestones in other places.

113

POST OFFICE CORNER, FELPHAM. More recent than most of the pictures, possibly as late as the 1950s. The street is still completely lacking in traffic, although a small group of villagers wait for the bus.

ST MARY'S CHURCH AND COTTAGES, FELPHAM, c. 1906. The church, which dates from the twelfth century, has two examples of Mass Dials. Before the use of clocks in the eighteenth century, these were the means by which the priests and villagers knew the times of the services (see also page 68).

114

'THE THATCHED HOUSE' AND LIMMER LANE, FELPHAM, 1930s. Here was Turret House, home of the poet William Hayley (1745-1820), which was demolished in 1961. Hayley was in some respects a somewhat sad figure. Even in his own lifetime he was known almost as much for his tendency to fall off the horses he rode, as for his serious literary work. There is also a grim legend concerning his second wife, which tells how, because of her insanity, he kept her chained up in the summerhouse.

CURIOSITY ROOM OF 'THE THATCHED HOUSE' INN, early 1900s. Like many country hostelries, it tried to attract custom by providing some unusual addition. Here it was a room full of unusual objects, such as a petrified coconut, a skeleton of a 28 year old lobster and a reproduction Moses in the Bull Rushes. Rather surprisingly, they found a buyer for these in 1915.

ADMIRALY ROAD, FELPHAM, *c.* 1911. In spite of the date on the card, the houses have a very 1930 'mock Tudor' look; but the road itself is very 1900, competely devoid of traffic and with the pedestrians walking down the centre.

FELPHAM BEACH, *c.* 1910. A relatively busy picture for the period, with its haystack and the coalman's cart loaded with sacks. Before the nineteenth century, most of the Felpham folk would have earned their living from either agriculture or fishing and this picture brings in both activities. It must have been a rather old fashioned village, as there are claims that it was the last place in Sussex where wife selling took place.

BEACH BUNGALOWS, FELPHAM, early 1900s. The bungalows are made from old railway carriages, but are much more attractive than in some other places. Gerard Young commented on 'The high platforms with verandahs and roof gardens, which in Summer are gay with flowers'

SLINDON VILLAGE, early 1900s. Once described as 'The most Sussex of Sussex villages', most of it is now owned by The National Trust; so it still retains much of the order and charm of past times.

HE POND, SLINDON.

SLINDON POND, early 1900s. The pond is probably as old as the village; its name was Weir Pond, as it was made by damming up an existing weir. As the picture shows, it was once used by carters and horses - and was also popular with small boys for fishing in Summer and skating in Winter. In December 1904, a youngster sailed across the pond in a tub with a stick for an oar. In 1860 a carter failed to stop his three horse timber wagon as it was coming down Church Hill, with it ending up crashing into the pond. The lead mare broke her back and it took the Slindon villagers three days to sort it all out. Jimmy Dean was a noted Slindon character, who contributed the Slindon Notes for the *West Sussex Gazette*, for almost forty years. His brother is the man with the reins in the cart beside the pond in this picture.

SLINDON WOODS, NEAR BOGNOR.

SLINDON WOODS, early 1900s. All the woods are named, such as Rough Wood; Hooks Wood; Eartham Wood; Dencher Wood; and Black Jack (once known as a smuggler's meeting place). Ghosts are supposed to frequent these woods. One is a riderless white horse, which is particulary frightening to real horses. Many old tales also survive and the old Gibbet, from which smugglers were hung, still stood on Slindon Common until the beginning of the present century. The story of 'Godiva of Slindon' is still told. Betty Thorpe loved a young Customs Officer - Will Garland. He was captured one day by a ruthless gang of smugglers, who declared they would whip him naked across the Common. Betsy offered herself in his place and that night the cruel leader of the gang, Ben Tapner, took her at her word. With her long flowing hair as her only covering, the girl was tied to a horse and lashed across the Common until she succumbed. Her lover Will was later shot by the smugglers, in trying to avenge her.

Dining Hall, New City, Middleton.

NEW CITY, MIDDLETON, *c.* 1922. After the First World War, a 'New City' model bungalow village was built here. It included a modern hotel of 200 bedrooms, tennis courts, its own dairy and farm and electric plant. Dubbed 'The Town of Never-mind' it was really a pioneer holiday camp, with a lot of novel ideas.

NEW CITY, MIDDLETON. MOTOR MUSICAL CHAIRS, *c.* 1922. One of the more unusual attractions staged for the visitors at this seaside village. Created by Sir Walter Blount, the site had been the Norman Thompson Flight Company flying-boat factory, during the First World War.

PAGHAM VILLAGE AND CHILDREN WITH PRAM, *c.* 1909. A vignette of past country life, with a prophetic link to the future, as in modern times the village has staged an annual pram race in aid of charity.

THE BEAR INN, PAGHAM. early 1900s. A small cottage-like pub, built in around 1840, taking delivery of its supplies. It was owned by the Turner family, who were also brewers. It was demolished in 1930 to be replaced by a more modern building.

NYTIMBER MILL, PAGHAM, c. 1905. The date of the building is uncertain, varying from 1762 to 1840. In 1845 the miller was William Adames and he was still there in 1887. It ceased working in 1916. Before the 1914/18 war, one of the sweeps was damaged by lightning and the timber needed to repair it had to come from Danzig. It was towed across the water by tug to Littlehampton harbour. The mill was badly damaged by fire in 1962.

PAGHAM BEACH AND BUS, 1950s. Once known as Selsey Haven, Pagham Harbour had been an important port. Old guide books always mention the famous 'Hushing Well'. This was a local attraction, with the sound of bursting bubbles on the surface of the water, like the simmering of a giant cauldron. During the 1939/45 war Pagham was host to the Free Norwegians, the beach being dubbed 'Little Norway'.

YAPTON VILLAGE, c. 1905. The best known local saying is that 'Those that come from Yapton do not shut doors'. There are several explanations for this, all equally unlikely. Perhaps one of the most possible it that smuggling was once rife in the village and that doors were left open to facilitate the smugglers in their unlawful, but not always unwelcome activities. Tradition says that contraband was often hidden inside two old table-like tombs in the churchyard. One Sunday a valuable cargo was also secreted beneath the pulpit, whilst the Vicar was actually preaching a sermon against the iniquity of smuggling.

YAPTON POST OFFICE, *c.* 1905. Up to 1923 the post office was a cottage with two steps up from the road. It also functioned as the village sweet shop. Yapton has been claimed as a place where wife selling was not uncommon. In 1898 in the local inn The Shoulder of Mutton and Cucumber, a thatcher named Marley sold his wife, child and furniture for seven shillings and sixpence and a quart of beer. The buyer was a ratcatcher named White. In the same year a villager is supposed to have sold his wife at the end of the harvest to a stranger for a mere three shillings.

HOLKHAM COTTAGES, *c.* 1907. These cottages were built by Sparkes, the local agricultural machinery proprietors, for their employees. The firm was once a very important employer in the village. The message on the card says, 'These are the houses where we live, but there are none of our children on it.'

BARNHAM MILL, early 1900s. This was built in 1829, replacing an earlier post mill. Just before the turn of the century, it was taken over by John Baker and remained in his family for many years. A Sussex directory of the period gives motive power as wind and steam, but by 1919 a gas engine had been fitted. Eventually the sweeps were removed. In its prime, eleven other working mills could be seen from the top of the mill. The children in the photograph would have attended schools at either Eastergate, Yapton or Walberton.

BARNHAM MILL, c. 1905. The owner's name is proudly displayed on the cart and the mill itself. Up to the 1930s the mill was a pretty sight with the white cap against the black of the tower and other parts painted red. During the 1939/45 war the army used it as a look-out post. Happily it is now being restored.

BARNHAM POST OFFICE, c. 1905. The postmaster, Mr Carpenter, was also a grocer and a coal merchant. The fine little baker's handcart, typical of the period, is lettered L. Bettesworth and Co., Yapton.

WALBERTON AND VILLAGERS, early 1900s. Nairn and Pevsner, in *The Buildings of England* (1965) speak of a 'charming long street'. The village pond has a tradition of never failing, although apparently it almost did in 1884.

HOLLY TREE INN AND POST OFFICE, WALBERTON, early 1900s. In 1903 the landlord of the inn was William Johnson. At the Post Office at the same time was Albert Paskett, sub-postmaster. Letters came from Arundel daily at 8 am and 12.45.

FLANSHAM POST OFFICE, 1950s. This is a small hamlet three miles from Bognor, without even a pub or a church. In 1828 a guide said that 'people in this favoured spot are remarkable for the amenity and cheerfulness in their manners'. The author Gerard Young obviously agreed with this, as he rented Meadow Cottage in Hoe Lane in 1938 for weekends and subsequently made a permanent home there.

GARDEN OF MEADOW COTTAGE, 1940. I started this book with a reference to Gerard Young, so it seems only right that I should end in the same way. This is the view from the winding path in the garden that he created in Flansham. Those who know his four books in which he described his life in the hamlet and his interest in all things Sussex, will recognise this picture. It is from his first book, *The Chronicle of a Country Cottage* (1942). He said his Lych Gate became a nine-day wonder, but eventually he felt it had been there for centuries.